Inspirational Buddhist Quotations

Meditations and Reflections

Book One

Oliver Kent

Dedicated with much affection to Lexi.

Introduction

You hold in your hands a blend of Buddhist wisdom. Some are poignant, others are serene, some will make you smile. Each is followed by a reflection or a **meditation**, though you are, of course, welcome to reflect on the meditations and meditate on the reflections.

Whether you read one a day, several at once, or jump around randomly, their beauty is that you can return to them time and again as they gradually reveal new insights.

They are also uplifting. At a time when we seem to be increasingly stressed and rushed, they remind us of the hope and love in the world.

So take a moment for yourself to savor this wisdom and listen to it calling you to awaken.

1

Our mind is the canvas on which the artists lay their color;

their pigments are our emotions;

their chiaroscuro the light of joy,

the shadow of sadness.

The masterpiece is of ourselves,

as we are of the masterpiece.

What would a painting of your Self look like? What are the emotions that you most often express? Would it be a picture filled with light and beauty, or would it be muddy colors and filled with grays and blacks?

Much like a real painting, you can continue to paint over what is there. A dark, fearful peace can be transformed into an expression of joy, one brushstroke at a time. Sometimes we look at ourselves and think that we cannot change, yet every moment offers us the opportunity to do so, to embrace love.

2

Respond to every call that excites your spirit.

When was the last time that you grew as a person? It doesn't have to be huge. A small step each day soon adds up. It's never too late to take another step.

3

Just as a candle cannot burn without fire, we cannot live without a spiritual life.

An innate part of being human is that we seek meaning, both in our lives and in the world around us. If we lose ourselves in the busyness of the day, our lives become smaller. We start to lose touch with that which is greater than us. We need to take time to listen to what inspires us to be better than what we are, to grow, and to become.

4

The emperor Goyozei was studying Zen under Gudo. He inquired, "In Zen, this very mind is Buddha. Is this correct?"

Gudo answered, "If I say yes, you will think that you understand without understanding. If I say no, I would be contradicting a fact which many understand quite well."

Logic only takes us so far. Then we have to let go of it. Rather than "working out" the answer like a maths problem, relax, sit with it, and listen.

5

Do not overrate what you have received, nor envy others. He who envies others does not obtain peace of mind.

We never really know the full picture of another's life. When we look at what others have received, we tend to imagine how our lives would be if we were in their place. But we don't know what else is going on in their lives, nor the way that they perceive themselves and the world around them.

A rich person is simply someone who spends less than they earn, whilst the poor person is one who spends more than they earned.

Whilst money is finite, there is an unlimited supply of love and beauty in the world. Indeed the more we experience and give love, the greater it becomes to all involved.

6

You are searching for treasure, but the real treasure is yourself.

The world of consumerism calls us to look outwards, distracting us with this and that. Yet all the joy and love and wisdom you possess are within you.

7

To be idle is a short road to death and to be diligent is a way of life,
foolish people are idle, wise people are diligent.

It's surprising how easy it is to drift in life. To wake up one day, look around, and wonder how you got here? Being mindful gives you more control over the path that you walk and the direction in which it takes you into life, better allowing you to have a life well-lived.

8

All conditioned things are impermanent.

This, too, will pass. Reflect on what will always be there. Breathe in the beauty of truth and love.

9

You will not be punished for your anger, you will be punished by your anger.

Being angry changes how you see the world. It filters your reality and how you see yourself and others. It changes the options that you see available to you and, in doing so, affects the path that you're walking. If all that you can see around you is colored by anger, then all that you will see are angry options.

Fear doesn't exist to make you afraid, fear is there to warn you of danger. Similarly, anger doesn't exist to make you angry, it's there to warn you when people are crossing your boundaries. It is like a candle that illuminates your room so that you can more clearly see what is happening. It's not there for you to use it to set fire to the room, yourself, or others!

10

The virtues, like the Muses, are always seen in groups. A good principle was never found solitary in any breast.

Rather than just focusing on love, also meditate on beauty and joy and peace. Let them dance together and be all the stronger in your life because of it.

11

Three things cannot be long hidden; the sun, the moon, and the truth.

Even though the sun and moon can be obscured by clouds, they still continue to exist. As day changes to night, though our ability to perceive them changes, they remain the same. The truth continues to be the truth throughout the ages. Some who have come before us stated this clearly, such as "things tend to fall down," while others spoke in such a way that you have to listen to the message between their words.

12

Let yourself be silently drawn by the stronger pull of what you really love!

There is and will only ever be 'one' you. No-one else can be you. Remember to be the best of you that you can be.

13

Those who are free of resentful thoughts surely find peace.

Too often, we think of someone correcting us in terms of punishment, either real or implied. And yet, ideally, correcting someone isn't about punishment at all. Quite the opposite, it's about preventing them from further suffering, especially further down their path.

Imagine a person on fire running down the street, crashing into people as they push them out of the way. The people that they crash into suffer various degrees of burns because of this. Some of them will yell at the person, others will simply stop to tend to their own injuries. Neither of these stops the person from being on fire and continuing to burn.

When someone causes us injury, be it physical, emotional, or psychological, we can find ourselves being resentful. But again, there is no need for this. The path that they are walking down leads them to greater suffering. There is no need for us to wish them further bad luck; they will do this to themselves through their actions. Indeed because of the nature of this, the suffering that they expose themselves to will come from another source, and so they will not seek recriminations against you.

The humane action is to try to calm them down long enough to put out the fire. Unfortunately, most of us lack this skill and, at best, encounter hostility and anger. When you view this in terms of trying to put out the fire, it's ridiculous. Would you say this to the firemen who were trying to put out a burning building? "How dare you extinguish this blaze and stop my house from burning down?!" But often, the person is so focussed on the fire that they can't pause long enough to listen.

Fortunately, we have a much safer option. We can choose to wish them well in the hope that our silent expression of love, even if done at a later time, may help them come to their senses and put out the fire. In doing so, we embrace love and so find peace.

14

There comes a time when nothing is meaningful except surrendering to love.

Look at the seemingly insignificant little wrongs that you do in your life. The ones that "don't really matter." What changes could you make so that you stop doing this?

15

Just as treasures are uncovered from the earth, so virtue appears from good deeds, and wisdom appears from a pure and peaceful mind. To walk safely through the maze of human life, one needs the light of wisdom and the guidance of virtue.

Although every vehicle comes with a manual that explains how it works and how to drive it, it would be madness to attempt to learn to drive purely by studying this book. We need to learn from experience to understand how our actions create our experiences.

Not everything goes as we expect, and often good intentions can go awry, but when we consistently choose love over hatred and fear, the lessons that we learn help us to gain greater insights into how to behave in a loving way, no matter the circumstances we may find ourselves in.

16

This is how I would die into the love I have for you - as pieces of cloud dissolve into the sunlight.

Each day, do one expression of love, even if it's smiling at a flower.

17

Even death is not to be feared by one who has lived wisely.

The fear of death often has its roots in regret of things done or not
done. When you can look back on a life well-lived, no matter how long
or short it may be, death is not something to fear.

We don't know what happens beyond death. Even those who have
attempted to describe it are trying to explain something beyond
human comprehension.

It's natural to fear the unknown, but to fear death, which is
inevitable, simply wears us down unnecessarily. We talk about animals
with claws worrying their prey. In that same way, worrying about death
gradually wears us down. It is better to focus on being mindful and be
present in the moment, living in love and harmony.

18

Be occupied with what you really value and let the thief take something else.

You only have so much time and energy throughout each day. Beware of wasting it or letting others drain you. Many have no interest in finding a better answer or traveling along the path, preferring to remain camped where they are and trying to trap you into staying there too. Offer them compassion and wish them well, but continue along your path.

19

The wise ones fashioned speech with their thought, sifting it as grain is sifted through a sieve.

We are living in a time of sound-bites, where often, for a thought to be listened to and considered, it must be as short and dramatic as possible. Instead of considering our thoughts before we speak them out loud, often we rush to proclaim whatever springs to mind.

Often we can feel that conversations are so frantic and that we are not being listened to, and so the only way to be heard is to speak the thoughts as soon as they occur to us. To pause and listen to the other person and then to take even more time to reflect on what they have said before considering our reply is becoming a dying art.

We are moving from a time where expertise was something that would be carefully acquired over many years and often have a recognizable title, such as a "Master artisan," to be willing to create our opinions in a matter of seconds and consider them to be of equal worth. We read a headline, or at most a paragraph, of an article and think ourselves fully informed on the matter.

We forget that there is no shame in not knowing. It is wiser to admit that you don't have all the information and expertise to remain open to the truth.

20

What matters is how quickly you do what your soul directs.

Look at your health, inner peace, and relationships. What can you do to strengthen them?

21

What we think, we become.

Where does inspiration come from? We can open ourselves up to its influence, but ultimately we don't have the final say on which new ideas spring into our minds. We can only decide whether we agree with them and wish to put them into practice.

However, most often, we receive inspiration related to what we think about. If we reflect on ways we can have better relationships with our friends, family, and community, we are far more likely to come up with new and better ways to do this. If we contemplate how to open ourselves to love through the way that we live our lives, then those insights gradually appear. Over time, our skills and expertise improve, and the quality of our inspirations improves.

But if we distract ourselves with worry and fear and hatred, cycling our thoughts in endless loops that go nowhere, we cut ourselves off from this and become stuck.

22

There can be no peace without, but through peace within. Society must be an expression of the souls of its members.

The next time you see an article with an inflammatory title, read it through until the end. If there are links, click on them. Do a quick online search. Get to the truth of the matter, rather than just reacting to it.

23

To live a pure unselfish life, one must count nothing as one's own in the midst of abundance.

If your life is truly abundant, then you are able to give away the things that you "own" because you will easily be able to get new ones. We talk of people who will "give you the shirt off their back," but this is much healthier for everyone involved if that person is immediately able to put on a new shirt.

To be abundant with love is to have access to an inexhaustible supply that you can freely give away, never becoming "poorer" for doing so.

24

You can search throughout the entire universe for someone who is more deserving of your love and affection than you are yourself, and that person is not to be found anywhere. You yourself, as much as anybody in the entire universe, deserve your love and affection.

The better we connect with love and, in doing so, love ourselves, the deeper we can love others. Pause and feel love flowing into and through you.

25

Chaos is inherent in all compounded things. Strive on with diligence.

Almost everything that we use has been made by many people. Often they have gone through many different designs, which in turn require modern tools, machinery, and materials.

So too, our ideas are filtered through a great many people. Someone will experience something, which they will then tell to someone else, who writes it up to go on the Internet or in a newspaper, but first, it's edited by another person to match a certain narrative.

Or someone listens to a partial explanation of a concept and then puts their own spin on it before presenting it to someone else, who in turn...

It's amazing how often an article will lead with a dramatic headline and act as if it's true in the first paragraph. But then, near the very end of the article, the author will admit that it's all nonsense, hoping that most people won't bother to read that far down. Or there may be a link that will explain how none of the headline is true, but again, most won't click on it to find out.

If an idea has passed through many hands, don't treat it the same as if it had passed through one.

26

Grief can be the garden of compassion. If you keep your heart open through everything, your pain can become your greatest ally in your life's search for love and wisdom.

Don't fall into the trap of being a fair-weather friend to Love. Practice being open and loving in the hard times so that when the hard times come again, you will be better able to stay in the moment and continue to feel love's presence.

27

Peace comes from within. Do not seek it without.

If you only experience peace as a reaction to your circumstances and environment, you will always be at the mercy of them. Once you learn how to attain peace within, then that is always present, regardless of your surroundings.

28

Your task is not to seek for love, but merely to seek and find all the barriers within yourself that you have built against it.

Think back to times when others have injured you and imagine them on fire, caused by their fear, anger, or hatred. Compassionately wish them well and hope that they manage to extinguish the flames. Then extinguish the fires within you.

29

I never see what has been done; I only see what remains to be done.

The past is the past. Remain in the present.

30

You know the value of every article of merchandise, but if you don't know the value of your own soul, it's all foolishness.

Breathe and be mindful. Let go of your ideas of who you are and take some time to just be.

31

It is better to conquer yourself than to win a thousand battles. Then the victory is yours. It cannot be taken from you, not by angels or by demons, heaven or hell.

The world around you is always changing. Even if you conquer something today, it will eventually change. Shelley's poem, "Ozymandius," tells of an Egyptian Pharoah who constructed a giant statue of himself, with the inscription:

"'My name is Ozymandias, king of kings:

Look on my works, ye Mighty, and despair!"

Unfortunately, now all that remains of his statue are a pair of giant feet.

When you grow as a person, that growth will always be a part of you, a foundation for further steps along the path.

32

I can see clouds a thousand miles away, hear ancient music in the pines.

Beauty is everywhere. Even the poorest man can see the sunset, watch the clouds dancing, and hear the pines singing in the wind.

33

The foot feels the foot when it feels the ground.

Much as the fish is unaware of the water in which it swims, often we aren't aware of something until it reacts to something else. Look around your life and ask yourself, "What if I no longer had this?" Take some time to appreciate what you have, but also to consider what you may be better off without.

34

I have no companion but Love, no beginning, no end, no dawn. The Soul calls from within me, 'You, ignorant of the way of Love, set Me free.'

When you feel love, stop and ask yourself, "What is my love calling me to do?"

35

Of those beings who live in ignorance, shut up and confined, as it were, in an egg, I have first broken the eggshell of ignorance and alone in the universe obtained the most exalted, universal Buddhahood.

Coming from anyone else other than the Buddha, this would seem a bit pretentious. Instead, it's a celebration of new possibilities. Rather than holding himself above others, he endeavored to help them to join him and attain enlightenment.

No matter how often you stumble, remember that there are those everywhere cheering you on, both in the now and throughout history. They quietly offer guidance through their words and deeds, which continue to echo long after they have passed by.

36

The moment I first heard love, I gave up my soul, my heart, and my eyes.

Love is beyond logic and knowledge. It can only be experienced. Don't try to trap it in a cage. Set it free and dance with it!

37

Ryokan, a Zen master, lived the simplest kind of life in a small hut at the foot of a mountain. One evening a thief visited the hut only to discover there was nothing to steal.

Ryokan returned and caught him.

"You have come a long way to visit me," he told the prowler, "and you should not return empty-handed. Please take my clothes as a gift."

The thief was bewildered. He took the clothes and slunk away. Meanwhile, Ryoken sat naked, watching the moon.

"Poor fellow," he thought, "I wish I could have given him this beautiful moon."

The thief is so focused on stealing what he considers to be valuable that he doesn't realize the value of what Ryoken is offering him. We, too, can fall into the trap of working desperately, whilst holding out for a holiday abroad, or a new car, or even just getting drunk at the weekend. The report we frantically scrabble together to meet the deadline, the rushed car journey home so that we're not too late for dinner, and so on. In doing so, we often forget to look around at other possibilities; to take the time to smell the flowers.

Mindfulness is always free. It doesn't even ask us to spend time; we can be mindful whilst we continue with our everyday lives.

38

He who walks in the eightfold noble path with unswerving

determination is sure to reach Nirvana.

Create a safety switch in your mind. When you feel anger, let it ound a mental alarm. Before you act, ask yourself, is anger helpful ere? If you're looking for a better answer, take a moment.

It may help to say this out loud, "Wait, give me a moment. I'm etting angry, and that's not what I want," as often the other person also getting angry and in now neither of you are striving for the uth.

39

Charity bestowed upon those who are worthy of it is like good seed sown on a good soil that yields an abundance of fruits. But alms given to those who are yet under the tyrannical yoke of the passions are like seed deposited in a bad soil. The passions of the receiver of the alms choke, as it were, the growth of merits.

We are all travelers through life, and as such, we can offer each other aid. However, you cannot control what someone chooses to do with your charity. Someone who is leading a positive and virtuous life will use your help to continue to do so and progress further along their path. Giving food to a food bank will most likely see it being given to those in need of food.

Whereas another person who is filled with fear and hate will use your aid to persist in that direction. A classic example is giving charity to a drug addict; they will most likely spend any money you give them on buying drugs rather than using it in an attempt at rehabilitation.

40

Water, stories, the body, all the things we do, are mediums that hide and show what's hidden.

What are the stories that speak to you? What do they have in common? What are they trying to tell you?

41

We are shaped by our thoughts; we become what we think. When the mind is pure, joy follows like a shadow that never leaves.

Our thoughts have tiny amounts of gravity and attract other similar thoughts. As they gather together, they start to influence us more and more to think in a certain way and begin creating new, similar thoughts, which in turn join the collection, increasing its gravity.

Then we start to think bigger and more intense thoughts along these lines; it's like the few initial pebbles falling down a mountain, gradually dislodging larger rocks until there is a full-blown avalanche.

When you are mindful, and your mind is filled with love, you naturally think thoughts of love and joy. They flow freely into your mind, throughout the day, like an unending mountain spring of pure water.

42

There is an invisible strength within us; when it recognizes two opposing objects of desire, it grows stronger.

Don't worry about achieving a state of no-mind. Just do it.

43

No one saves us but ourselves. No one can, and no one may. We ourselves must walk the path.

Although others can help us to help ourselves, ultimately, we must make the choice to accept and act on this help. Indeed, often the first step is simply to ask for help.

44

Let my skin and sinews and bones dry up, together with all the flesh and blood of my body! I welcome it! But I will not move from this spot until I have attained the supreme and final wisdom.

When you next find yourself about to kill time, instead take that moment to be mindful

45

The mind is everything. What you think you become.

Often, we think of meditation as something you do to generate a bit of peace in your life for a few moments, rather than a way of being which has a profound effect on your life. It is important to take the time to become better at being mindful until you are able to sustain it through most of your waking day.

46

Life is swept along, next-to-nothing its span. For one swept to old age, no shelters exist. Perceiving this danger in death, one should drop the world's bait and look for peace.

If someone were to write a novel or make a film based on your thoughts, what genre would it be? A romance, horror, mystery, or something else? What do you want it to be?

47

Listen! Clam up your mouth and be silent like an oyster shell, for that tongue of yours is the enemy of the soul, my friend. When the lips are silent, the heart has a hundred tongues.

When we think we know the answer, sometimes we forget that there are better answers. We stop looking and instead delight in sharing how we have found the truth with those around us. In doing so, we focus on the words rather than the music between the words. We forget to listen with our hearts and open ourselves up to a deeper understanding.

48

Unknown is the length of life.

Modern life seems to alternate between stress and boredom. We peak of "killing time."

We'll be happy when we pass our exams, when we graduate niversity, when we get a job, when we get promoted, when we etire...

At the rate we're going, we'll have one perfect day just before we ie! "I'll be happy when" assumes that we have a long life ahead of s. But tomorrow is promised to no-one. Pause and ask yourself, why ot be happy now?

49

This is the path to purity.

If something is impure, it contains things that it shouldn't. Purity comes from letting go of what is not needed in our lives, minds, and hearts, rather than accumulating more.

50

Something opens our wings. Something makes boredom and hurt disappear. Someone fills the cup in front of us. We taste only sacredness.

Love is abundant, infinite, and freely available to us. We have only to open ourselves up to it. When we speak of holiness, we are speaking of that which makes us whole again; this happens when we are filled with love.

51

That which is false troubles the heart, but truth brings joyous tranquility.

We can try to convince ourselves that something is true, even when deep down, we know that it isn't, but our heart warns us of the deception and calls to us to let it go and seek the truth.

When we discover something that is true, then our heart rejoices!

When we are thirsty, if we eat salty food, rather than drinking, our body tells us that we are still thirsty; yet when we finally drink water, then it refreshes us.

In the same way, our hearts continually thirst for love and the truth

52

There are a thousand ways to kneel and kiss the ground; there are a thousand ways to go home again.

There is no monopoly on the truth. There is no one right way. We are blessed in that rather than having to find the exact footsteps, like stepping stones across a pond, there are many ways in which we can travel along the way, returning to who we were before we were born.

53

Everyone has been made for some particular work, and the desire for that work has been put in every heart.

I am continually amazed that there are people who enjoy proofreading. And doubtless, there are people who are amazed that I enjoy writing. By combining our many talents, we come together as a society to be greater than the sum of its parts. The challenge for many is to find what they love. This doesn't have to be your career. A writer may be content to blog for free while continuing their day job as a grocer.

Find what calls to you, what you love, what inspires you, and then, in some way, do that work, make the world a better place.

54

There is also a heaven upon earth in our own breasts. Do not seek it without, but within your heart; then you will not come into heaven for the first time when you die, but remain in it always.

What do you know to be true? Reflect on the times your mind was clouded and remember that mindfulness helps to clear confusion away.

55

It is a man's own mind, not his enemy or foe, that lures him to evil ways.

Often we think of ourselves as reacting to other people and our surroundings, "He made me do it," and so forth.

However, if it were possible to make someone act in a certain way, merely by saying certain things, then Buddhist monks would spend their whole lives walking around the world, saying those things that cause immediate enlightenment, to everyone that they meet.

56

Sunlight fell upon the wall; the wall received a borrowed splendor. Why set your heart on a piece of earth, O simple one? Seek out the source which shines forever.

What brings you joy? It doesn't matter if it's "important" or "silly" not what grown-ups/men/women should do. Put aside some time d energy to nurture this.

57

To enjoy good health, to bring true happiness to one's family, to bring peace to all, one must first discipline and control one's own mind. If a man can control his mind, he can find the way to Enlightenment, and all wisdom and virtue will naturally come to him.

Your mind is the lens through which you see the world. If your mind twists reality into nightmares while it crashes about and makes you afraid or hateful, that will have a massive impact on your life.

However, if you see the world through the lens of love, and your mind is calm and peaceful, then your path will be filled with grace.

58

Beauty surrounds us, but usually, we need to be walking in a garden to know it.

Imagine sitting in a Buddhist monastery high in the Himalayas. Outside is cold and ice. What would you miss about the life you have now?

59

Hatred does not cease by hatred, but only by love; this is the eternal rule.

Whatever words we utter should be chosen with care, for people will hear them and be influenced by them for good or ill.

When a parent strikes a child whilst telling them "don't hit your sister," they are telling the child that the parent is to be obeyed, not because they are right, but because they are more powerful. When the child grows up and becomes bigger and stronger than their parents, this can backfire tragically.

If a person is on fire, how will you extinguish the flames by pouring gasoline over them?

60

Your sadness is connected to your insolence and refusal to praise.

What have you received today that brought you joy? Share it with others.

61

Virtue is persecuted more by the wicked than it is loved by the good.

It can be tempting to say that virtue is something to be aspired to rather than something to be actually achieved in your daily life. This becomes a problem when you encounter those who are behaving in a virtuous manner throughout their normal lives.

Many then seek to either dismiss them, perhaps saying that they are only behaving in this way because they expect some sort of reward, possibly in the after-life. Or they come up with reasons as to why these people are "special," such as the Dalai Lama, and so the standards that they live to shouldn't apply to "ordinary people."

Virtuous people don't tend to think of themselves that way. They just think of what they are doing as "living."

62

By ourselves is evil done, By ourselves we pain endure, By ourselves we cease from wrong, By ourselves become we pure. No one saves us but ourselves. No one can, and no one may. We ourselves must walk the path. Buddhas only show the way.

Before making big decisions, take some time to be mindful. With practice, move onto being mindful when making smaller decisions.

63

I do not believe in a fate that falls on men however they act; but I d believe in a fate that falls on them unless they act.

We all have choices throughout our lives, and they each influence the path that we walk.

We have some say in the outcome. How much of this is fate is open to discussion. But most people will say that at least half of what happens is due to your actions, whilst the other half is due to luck and to those things outside of your control.

However, if you do nothing, then your effect on the outcome is also nothing, leaving your fate purely down to luck.

64

Don't grieve. Anything you lose comes round in another form.

Imagine fear and grief as a giant cat worrying you with its paws. See the futility of doing this to yourself. Stop worrying yourself.

65

He who gives away shall have real gain. He who subdues himself shall be free; he shall cease to be a slave of passions. The righteous man casts off evil, and by rooting out lust, bitterness, and illusion do we reach Nirvana.

Often we think of positive things in terms of gain. How do you get "happy"? And in doing so, sometimes we are blinded to the possibility that the answer is by letting go.

The Aztecs believed that every object had a spirit, which had to be regularly prayed to in order to keep it appeased. As such, they thought carefully every time they wanted a new possession.

Imagine the amount of "stuff" you have; what if you had to say a prayer for every single piece, every day! You probably wouldn't have time for anything else.

In the same way, look at the habits you have in your life and how much time and energy they take up. By letting go of the ones that drain you and waste your energy, you can better use it elsewhere in your life.

66

Those who have come to be, those who will be. All will go, leaving the body behind. The skillful person, realizing the loss of all, should live the holy life ardently.

Look at your life. Are you where you expected to be? Where would you like to be in a year's time? Five years? What direction do you need to head in order to get there?

67

Do not dwell in the past, do not dream of the future, concentrate the mind on the present moment.

The past is gone, and the future has yet to happen. All they can do is istract us from the now.

68

If you find the mirror of the heart dull, the rust has not been cleared
from its face.

Sometimes life can wear us down. When this happens, take some time to experience love and beauty in your life. The rust can always be cleared away, letting the mirror shine again.

69

To keep the body in good health is a duty... otherwise we shall not be able to keep our mind strong and clear.

While not impossible, it's certainly harder to be mindful and present in the moment when you are in poor health and the moment is unpleasant. Better to stay in good health, especially being aware of the cumulative effect of the small choices in your life; too many late nights and early mornings, too much junk food, and too little time to stop and breathe.

70

Lovers don't finally meet somewhere. They're in each other all along.

Find someone with whom you can talk to and actually pause before you reply. Savor this. The conversation becomes like a good meal, rather than gobbling down fast food.

71

You, yourself, as much as anybody in the entire universe, deserve your love and affection.

"Love your neighbor" often leaves out the important part of loving yourself as well. It's worth asking yourself, "Am I treating myself in a loving way? Would I treat someone else this way, particularly if they were a child?"

We can fall into the habit of berating and doubting ourselves, thinking, "If only...." Remember that you deserve your own compassion.

72

The gifts of lovers to one another are, in respect to love, nothing but forms; yet, they testify to invisible love.

We are all expressions of love. We live in a world of lovers. Remember this.

73

Thousands of candles can be lit from a single candle without shortening the life of the candle. Sharing Happiness never lessens it.

Puppies are the ultimate expression of this. They cheerfully share their happiness with anyone and, in doing so, multiply it exponentially for all involved. In the world that tells you that to be happy, you must buy this phone, or these shoes, remember that happiness is all around you and can be freely shared.

74

By embracing anger, you are like a man who wants to strike another and picks up a burning ember or excrement in his hand and so first burns himself or makes himself stink.

When was the last time felt anger? Ask yourself, "What was my anger warning me of?"

75

However many holy words you read, however many you speak, what good will they do you if you do not act on upon them?

Life is the ultimate practical exam. It doesn't matter how good you are in theory, it's how well you can perform.

76

Let the beauty of what you love be what you do.

Look for Happiness. The more you look, the more you'll see it, hiding in plain sight. Share it with others!

77

There are only two mistakes one can make along the road to truth;
not going all the way and not starting.

Be careful of falling into the trap of thinking that you have walked far enough along the path and that now you understand the truth, or at least what you understand is "good enough." Keep looking for the deeper truth.

78

Love will find its way through all languages on its own.

What is there in your life that feeds your heart? What makes you feel love and causes you to love others in return?

Perhaps you used to have this in your life but somehow lost it along the way? Maybe friends moved to another state or country, or your life became too busy.

Ask yourself how you can reconnect to these sources of love in your life.

79

Better than a thousand hollow words is one word that brings peace.

Sometimes, we forget that amongst the noise of cleverness and latitudes, a simple word spoken from the heart can be a far greater source of peace and comfort.

80

Everything that is made beautiful and fair and lovely is made for the
eye of one who sees.

**Put aside a moment of each day to be yourself, to open up to
Universe. To remember that love is infinite and to bask in that joy.**

81

The only real failure in life is not to be true to the best one knows.

We never really know the full impact that our actions have. Like the butterfly flapping its wings and causing a hurricane halfway across the world, the best we can do is to act in the best way we know how; an important aspect of this is the willingness to question, to seek better answers, and to change as we do so.

82

The garden of love is green without limit and yields many fruits other than sorrow or joy. Love is beyond either condition; without spring, without autumn, it is always fresh.

Take a moment and accept that there are things that are simply beyond your ability to fully understand, and that's ok.

Open yourself to love.

83

In a controversy, the instant we feel anger, we have already ceased striving for the truth and have begun striving for ourselves.

The Greeks favored the idea that each person should choose one side of an argument and defend it against each other, whilst at the same time, attacking them. The problem with this is that it assumes one of you has the right answer. If one of you argues that two plus two equals five, while the other says that two plus two equals three, it doesn't really matter which one of you "wins" the argument.

It's far more constructive if you both look for a better answer than the one that you have. Rather than taking sides, you both cooperate with each other. When you do this, there is no anger because you are simply looking for the truth. The truth is. It does not belong to any one person. When you find it, you both benefit.

84

Turn away from what is unwholesome and ill.

You are a work of art. How can you live so that you continue to become more beautiful and have a deeper expression of love?

85

Health is the greatest gift, contentment the greatest wealth,

faithfulness the best relationship.

These are all the things that we tend to notice when they are missing. It's better to dig your well before you're thirsty and act in ways that will naturally keep bringing these things to you.

86

Through Love, all that is bitter will be sweet, Through Love, all that is copper will be gold, Through Love, all dregs will become wine, through Love, all pain will turn to medicine.

For all the attraction that wealth holds out to us, true riches come from love.

87

Unity can only be manifested by the Binary. Unity itself and the idea of Unity are already two.

Often there are things that refuse to fit into boxes we cleverly make out of words. We know when something is beautiful and when we are in the presence of beauty, but we cannot ever truly capture in words a definition of what beauty is.

The same applies to being one with creation. To be aware of the concept means that we have become distinct and separate in order to do so.

88

When you see love with all your heart, you shall find its echoes in the universe.

Remember a time when you felt love. How did you see the world through its lens?

89

A jug fills drop by drop.

A lot of our life simply runs on habit. We do "this" because we've always done "this." But it's such a small thing, so we tell ourselves it doesn't really matter, we can change it anytime we want. In fact, someday we will when we've just got a bit more time. For now, we need to focus on the more important things, keeping our heads above water in an increasingly frantic world.

While those small things are easy to change at first, they become harder over time as the jug fills. Imagine if you had to empty the jug one drop at a time?

There is a story of two men who seek forgiveness. One has only done small wrongs throughout his life, and the other one has committed a single significant wrong. The monk tells them to go and gather up a stone to represent each wrong and bring it back to him. One man brings back a huge rock, while the other returns with a hundred pebbles. "Excellent," the monk replies, "now to be forgiven, simply put them back where you found them."

In the same way, it becomes increasingly easy to forget the little things that we did that somehow became the ingrained habits of how you act today.

90

Be warmed with love, for only love exists. Where is intimacy except in giving and receiving?

Take a moment and remember that you are a conduit for love. It ows through you to and from others.

91

When one has the feeling of dislike for evil, when one feels tranquil
one finds pleasure in listening to good teachings; when one has these
feelings and appreciates them, one is free of fear.

The more that you embrace love in your life, the easier and more
natural it becomes. You see the world as a kinder, more benevolent
place, filled with beauty and possibilities. At the same time, fear and
hatred feel increasingly unnatural and indeed become harder.

92

Find the sweetness in your own heart, that you may find the sweetness in every heart.

Take a moment right now and breathe.

93

A student once asked, "If I haven't anything in my mind, what shall I do?"

Joshu replied, "Throw it out."

"But if I haven't anything, how can I throw it out?" continued the questioner.

"Well," said Joshu, "then carry it out."

The state of "no-mind" isn't something that we can maintain permanently throughout our lives. We dip in and out of it, only realizing that we have attained it after we have left it again. So there's no need to worry about being stuck in a state of no-mind for the rest of your life.

94

Close your eyes. Fall in love. Stay there.

Look back over the last five years. What are the thoughts you had most often, indeed so often, that they have become habits? Are they serving you? Do they help you walk along your path?

95

The foolish man conceives the idea of 'self.' The wise man sees there is no ground on which to build the idea of 'self;' thus, he has a right conception of the world and well concludes that all compounds amassed by sorrow will be dissolved again, but the truth will remain.

Who were you before you were born? Are you the same person now that you were as a child? The person that we perceive ourselves to be is an illusion of our own creation. It changes over time; sometimes drastically due to our circumstances; if we define ourselves by our work, what happens if we are fired or change careers? If we define ourselves by our relationships, what happens when those end or change?

"Who am I?" is most often defined in reaction to the situation we find ourselves in. The brightest student in a school may suddenly find themselves merely average when they go to university.

No matter who you are or who you were, that image of self will eventually cease to exist, except in memory.

Much of the pain we experience in life comes from the conflict between how we see ourselves and our circumstances, particularly in the mirror of others' reactions to us.

By remembering that this "self" is just a temporary, shorthand expression, we can relax and take a step back. When there is no self, there is simply eternity.

96

Love is the vital core of the soul. And of all you see, only love is infinite.

What is abundant in your life? What can you immediately replace No matter how poor you are, there is always an endless supply of love and joy at your fingertips.

97

With fools, there is no companionship. Rather than to live with men who are selfish, vain, quarrelsome, and obstinate, let a man walk alone.

The Internet has made it increasingly easy to attract the attention of toxic people. Simply state any opinion as honestly as you can; you can say that puppies are adorable, and there will be those who agree and those who disagree, regardless of what you said.

It's important to distinguish between those who genuinely support you and those who are simply making noise to attract attention. The latter isn't looking to help you along your path or to be there when you need them. If anything, they can distract you from being yourself and drain your energies in the process.

98

In silence, there is eloquence.

Learn how to trust in not thinking. Just open your heart.

99

We are what we think. All that we are arises with our thoughts.
With our thoughts, we make the world.

It's easy to think that everybody sees the world and the same way that we do, but you only have to look at the strident discussions on politics to see that this clearly isn't the case. We each view the world through the lens of our thoughts, editing it to suit our beliefs. We exaggerate the things that we like and agree with that, while we lessen the importance of things that we disagree with.

There is a cyclic relationship between our thoughts and our beliefs. Our thoughts create our beliefs, but at the same time, our beliefs influence our thoughts.

We can take back control of this relationship by being mindful of our thoughts and how they influence the world as we see it.

If our thoughts are filled with negativity, we see the world as a darker, lonelier place. Whereas if our thoughts are filled with love, we see the world around us has been filled with delight and hope.

100

It may be that the satisfaction I need depends on my going away so that when I've gone and come back, I'll find it at home.

We can fail to appreciate what we have until it is gone. Sometimes we need to lose it or to move further away to gain the necessary perspective to fully appreciate it. In order to really see your house, you have to first go outside.

Made in the USA
Monee, IL
15 March 2021